How Can We Have Faith?

GW00771400

Booklets taken from Questions of Life:

Is There More to Life Than This?

Who Is Jesus?

Why Did Jesus Die?

How Can We Have Faith?

Why and How Do I Pray?

Why and How Should I Read the Bible?

How Does God Guide Us?

The Holy Spirit

How Can I Resist Evil?

Why and How Should I Tell Others?

Does God Heal Today?

What About the Church?

How Can I Make the Most of the Rest of My Life?

How Can We Have Faith?

NICKY GUMBEL

Contents

How Can We Have Faith?

Some people are at their best in the morning, others come to life at night. My best time of day is first thing. I wake up full of energy but as the day goes on I begin to fade. By nine o'clock at night I am ready to go to bed. By ten o'clock I am falling asleep. By eleven o'clock I am asleep, wherever I happen to be!

"Midnight feasts aren't his thing."

I have always been like that, even when I was at university. At the end of my last term there I attended our college ball. That evening I met a girl whom I had talked to a couple of times before. She was about the same age as me. We started chatting and then we danced. Eleven o'clock came and went. Three o'clock came and went. Five o'clock came and went. At seven o'clock in the morning we started playing tennis. Then we went boating on the river and afterwards had lunch. I hadn't had a moment's sleep, but I didn't feel remotely tired. Word quickly spread among my friends that I was definitely going to marry this girl because I had been up after eleven o'clock at night. And they were right – Pippa and I were married two years later!

That night a new life had begun – I was never the same again. Similarly, becoming a Christian is the start of a new life. Relationships are exciting but the most exciting relationship of all is our relationship with God. As Paul wrote, 'those who become Christians become new persons. They are not the same any more for the old is gone. A new life has begun!' (2 Corinthians 5:17, NLT). I sometimes keep a note of what people say or write after they have begun the new life that Paul is speaking about. For example:

> I now have hope where previously there was only despair. I can forgive now, where before there was only coldness… God is so alive for

me. I can feel him guiding me and the complete and utter loneliness which I have been feeling is gone. God is filling a deep, deep void.

I had met other Christians (through a friend) who just seemed very at peace with the world and fulfilled and I thought I fancy a bit of that... I found God and became a Christian during Alpha... I feel at peace and happier with life and am searching for ways to strengthen my relationship with God.

When St Paul refers to people becoming Christians, what does he mean? What is a Christian? The word Christian, of course, can be used in many different ways in our society. However, originally a Christian was a *Christ*ian, a follower of Jesus: someone who has a relationship with God through his son.

Experiences of how that relationship begins vary greatly. Some people know the exact date on which they became a Christian, as I do. Some would say, 'I can never remember a time when I wasn't a Christian.' Others might say, 'I think there was a time when I wasn't a Christian. I am a Christian now, but it was a process and I couldn't tell you exactly when it happened.' What matters is not so much the experience as the fact that when we receive Christ, we become a child of God. As the apostle John writes, 'Yet to all who received him, to those who believed in his name, he gave the right to become children of God' (John 1:12). Let us use this analogy: on a train from Paris to Berlin, some people will be awake at the moment the train crosses the border. These passengers will know the exact moment that it happened. Others will be asleep. What matters is that they know they've arrived in Berlin.

Many people are uncertain about whether they are Christians or not. I ask people at the end of Alpha to fill in questionnaires. One of the questions I ask is, 'Would you have described yourself as a Christian at the beginning of Alpha?' Here is a list of some of the answers:

'Yes, but without any real experience of a relationship with God.'

'Sort of.'

'Possibly yes/think so.'

'Not sure.'

'Probably.'

'Ish.'

'Yes – though looking back possibly no.'

'No, a semi-Christian.'

The New Testament makes it clear that it is possible for us to be sure that we are Christians and that we have eternal life. The apostle John writes, 'I write these things to you who believe in the name of the Son of God so that you may *know* that you have eternal life' (1 John 5:13, italics mine).

How can we know that we have been given eternal life? Just as three legs support a camera tripod, the assurance of our relationship with God stands firmly based on the activity of all three members of the Trinity: the promises which the Father gives us in his word, the sacrifice of the Son for us on the cross and the assurance of the Spirit in our hearts. These can be summarised under three headings: the word of God, the work of Jesus and the witness of the Holy Spirit.

The word of God

If you asked me how I know I'm married, one answer I could give would be to show you a particular document – our marriage certificate. This is a piece of evidence that proves the fact that Pippa and I are married. If you asked me how I know I am a Christian, one answer I could give would be to show you a document – the Bible.

The first leg of the tripod is the word of God. Our knowledge of God is based on the promises in the Bible. It is based on facts, not feelings. If we were to rely only on our feelings we could never be sure about anything. Our feelings go up and down depending on all sorts of factors, such as the weather or what we've had for breakfast. They can be changeable and even deceptive. The promises in the Bible, which is the word of God, do not change and are totally reliable.

There are many great promises in the Bible. A verse that I found helpful, especially at the beginning of my Christian life, is one that comes in the last book of the Bible. In a vision St John sees Jesus speaking to seven different churches. To the church in Laodicea Jesus says: 'Here I am! I stand at the door and knock. If anyone hears my voice and opens the door, I will come in and eat with them, and they with me' (Revelation 3:20).

There are many ways of speaking about starting the new life of the Christian faith – 'becoming a Christian', 'giving our lives to Christ', 'receiving Christ', 'inviting Jesus into our lives', 'believing in him' and 'opening the door to Jesus' are some of the variations. All of them describe the same reality; that Jesus enters our lives by the Holy Spirit, as is pictured in this verse.

The Pre-Raphaelite artist, Holman Hunt (1827–1910), inspired by this verse, painted *The Light of the World*. He painted three versions in all. One hangs in Keble College, Oxford; another version is in the Manchester City Art Gallery; the most famous toured the world in 1905–1907 and was presented to St Paul's Cathedral in June 1908, where it still hangs. When the first version was shown it received generally poor reviews. Then, on 5 May 1854, John Ruskin, the artist and critic, wrote to *The Times* and explained the symbolism at length and brilliantly defended it as 'one of the very noblest works of sacred art ever produced in this or any other age'.

Jesus, the Light of the World, stands at a door, which is overgrown with ivy and weeds. The door represents the door of someone's life. This person has never invited Jesus to come into his or her life. Jesus is standing at the door and knocking. He is awaiting a response. He wants to come in and be part of that person's life. Apparently, someone said to Holman Hunt that he had made a mistake. They told him, 'You have forgotten to paint a handle on the door.'

'Oh no,' replied Hunt, 'that is deliberate. There is only one handle and that is on the inside.'

In other words, we have to open the door to let Jesus into our lives. Jesus will never force his way in. He gives us the freedom to choose. It is up to us whether or not we open the door to him. If we do, he promises, 'I will come in and eat with them and they with me.' Eating together is a sign of the friendship which Jesus offers to all those who open the door of their lives to him.

Once we have invited Jesus to come in, he promises that he will never leave us. He says to his disciples, 'I am with you always' (Matthew 28:20). We may not always be in direct conversation with him, but he will always be there. If you are working in a room with a friend, you may not be talking to each other all the time, but you are nevertheless aware of each other's presence. This is how it is with the presence of Jesus. He is with us always.

This promise of the presence of Jesus with us is closely related to another extraordinary promise, which comes in the New Testament. Jesus promises to give his followers eternal life (John 10:28). As we have seen, 'eternal life' in the New Testament is a quality of life that comes from being in a relationship with God through Jesus Christ (John 17:3). It starts now, when we experience the fullness of life which Jesus came to bring (John 10:10). Yet it is not just for this life; it goes on into eternity.

The resurrection of Jesus from the dead has many implications. First, it assures us about the *past*, that what Jesus achieved on the cross was effective. 'The resurrection is not the reversal of a defeat, but the proclamation of a victory.'[1] Second, it assures us about the *present*: Jesus is alive. His power is with us, bringing us life in all its fullness. Third, it assures us about the *future*. This life is not the end; there is life beyond the grave. History is not meaningless or cyclical; it is moving towards a glorious climax.

One day Jesus will return to earth to establish a new heaven and a new earth (Revelation 21:1). Then those who are in Christ will go to 'be with the Lord for ever' (1 Thessalonians 4:17). There will be no more crying, for there will be no more pain. There will be no more temptation, for there will be no more sin. There will be no more suffering and no more separation from loved ones. Then we will see Jesus face to face

(1 Corinthians 13:12). We will be given glorious and painless resurrection bodies (1 Corinthians 15). We will be transformed into the moral likeness of Jesus Christ (1 John 3:2). Heaven will be a place of intense joy and delight which goes on for ever. Some have ridiculed this by suggesting it would be monotonous or boring. But: 'No eye has seen, no ear has heard, no mind has conceived what God has prepared for those who love him' (1 Corinthians 2:9 quoting Isaiah 64:4).

As C. S. Lewis put it in one of his Narnia books:

> The term is over: the holidays have begun. The dream is ended: this is the morning... all their life in this world... had only been the cover and the title page: now at last they were beginning Chapter One of the Great Story which no one on earth has read: which goes on forever: in which every chapter is better than the one before.[2]

The work of Jesus

To the question how do I know I'm married, I could show you the marriage certificate. I could also point you to an event that took place on 7 January 1978, our wedding. Similarly, if you asked me how I know I'm a Christian, I could also point to an event in history; the death and resurrection of Jesus Christ.

Therefore, the second leg of the tripod is the work of Jesus. The wonderful news is that our confidence in eternal life is based not on what we do or achieve, but on what Jesus has done for us. What he did on the cross enables us to receive eternal life as a gift (John 10:28). We do not earn a gift. We accept it with gratitude.

It all starts with God's love for us: 'For God so loved the world that he gave his one and only Son, that whoever believes in him shall not perish but have eternal life' (John 3:16). We all deserve to 'perish'. God, in his love for us, saw the mess we were in and gave his only Son, Jesus, to die for us. As a result of his death, everlasting life is offered to all who believe.

On the cross, Jesus took all our wrong doing upon himself. This had been clearly prophesied in the Old Testament. In the book of Isaiah, written hundreds of years beforehand, the prophet foresaw what 'the suffering servant' would do for us and said: 'We all, like sheep, have gone astray, each of us has turned to our own way; and the Lord has laid on him [ie Jesus] the iniquity of us all' (Isaiah 53:6).

What the prophet is saying is that we have all done wrong – we have all gone astray. He says elsewhere that the things that we do wrong cause a separation between us and God (Isaiah 59:1–2). This is one of the reasons why God can seem remote. There is a barrier between us and him which prevents us from experiencing his love.

On the other hand, Jesus never did anything wrong. He lived a perfect life. There was no barrier between him and his Father. On the cross, God transferred our wrong doings ('our iniquity') onto Jesus ('the Lord has laid on him the iniquity of us all'). That is why Jesus cried out on the cross, 'My God, my God, why have you forsaken me?' (Mark 15:34). At that moment he was cut off from God – not because of his own wrong doing, but because of ours.

I am slightly cynical when I hear of a 'free gift'. Eternal life is a free gift unlike any other and although free for us, it cost Jesus his life. We receive this gift through repentance and faith.

What is repentance? The Greek word for 'repentance' means changing our minds. If we want to receive this gift, we have to be willing to turn from everything we know to be wrong. These are the things which do us harm and lead to 'death' (Romans 6:23a). C. S. Lewis said repentance was like 'laying down your arms, surrendering, saying you are sorry, realising that you have been on the wrong track and being ready to start life over again from the ground floor'.

What is faith? Blondin was a famous tightrope walker and acrobat in the nineteenth century. Large crowds used to watch him, particularly when he was crossing the Niagara Falls. His act began with a relatively simple crossing using a balancing pole. Then he would throw the pole away and begin to amaze the onlookers. There is the story of an occasion when a royal party from Britain went to watch him perform. He crossed the tightrope on stilts, then blindfolded; next he stopped halfway to cook and eat an omelette. He then wheeled a wheelbarrow from one side to the other as the crowd cheered. He put a sack of potatoes into the wheelbarrow and wheeled that across. The crowd cheered louder. Then he approached the royal party and asked the Duke of Newcastle, 'Do you believe that I could take a man across the tightrope in this wheelbarrow?'

'Yes, I do,' said the Duke.

'Hop in!' replied Blondin. The crowd fell silent, but the Duke of Newcastle would not accept his challenge. No one was willing to volunteer. Eventually, an old woman stepped out of the crowd and climbed into the wheelbarrow. Blondin wheeled her all the way across and all the way back. The old woman was Blondin's mother, the only person willing to put her life in his hands. Faith in this sense is 'hopping in'. It isn't merely an intellectual exercise; it involves an active step of putting our trust in Jesus.

When we repent and believe, we can be sure of God's forgiveness and know our guilt has been taken away. We can also be sure that we will never be condemned. As Paul puts it, 'Therefore, there is now no condemnation for those who are in Christ Jesus' (Romans 8:1). This, then, is the second reason we can be sure that we have eternal life – because of what Jesus achieved for us on the cross by dying for us.

The witness of the Spirit

To prove that I am married, as well as a document and an event, I could also point you to the experience of many years of marriage. To show how I know I am a Christian I can point to a document, to an event that took place in history, and third to the experience of the Holy Spirit. When someone becomes a Christian, God's Holy Spirit comes to live within them. There are two aspects of this experience that help us to be sure of our faith in Christ.

First, he transforms us from within. He produces the character of Jesus in our lives. This is called 'the fruit of the Spirit' – 'love, joy, peace, patience, kindness, goodness, faithfulness, gentleness and self-control' (Galatians 5:22–23). When the Holy Spirit comes to live within us this 'fruit' begins to grow.

There will be changes in our character that should be observable by other people, but obviously these changes do not occur overnight. We once planted a pear tree in our garden and almost every day I used to look excitedly to see if any fruit had appeared. One day a friend of mine (the illustrator of this book) hung a large Granny Smith apple on the tree with a piece of string. Upon closer examination, even I was not fooled by this! From my limited knowledge of gardening I know that fruit takes time to grow and pear trees do not produce apples. It's over a period of time that the Holy Spirit transforms us to be more loving, more joyful, more peaceful, more patient, more kind, more self-controlled.

As well as changes in our character there should be changes in our relationships, both with God and with other people. We develop a new love for God – Father, Son and Holy Spirit. For example, hearing the word 'Jesus' has a different emotional impact. Before I was a Christian, to me, the word 'Jesus' was just a swear word. If I heard his name on the radio or on the television I would usually switch channels, as I was not very interested in religion. After I became a Christian, however, I would turn it up because my attitude to Jesus had completely changed. This was a little sign of my new love for him.

Our attitude to others also changes. Often, new Christians say that they begin to notice the faces of people in the street and on the bus. Before, they had little interest; now they feel sympathy for people who look sad or lonely. I found that one of the biggest differences was in my attitude to other Christians. Before, I tended to avoid anyone who had a Christian faith. Afterwards, I found they weren't as bad as I had expected! Indeed, I started to experience a depth of friendship with other Christians that I had never known in my life before.

Second, the Holy Spirit also brings an inner experience of God. He creates a deep, personal conviction that we are children of God (Romans 8:15–16).

I have three children, who are now grown up. In my opinion many children are overworked during their time at school. The main advice I used to give my children was, 'Don't work so hard!' Whatever was said in my children's school reports, I thought they were fantastic. I remember looking at my thirteen-year-old daughter's report, which I (of course) thought was wonderful. She, however, pointed out areas in which she was disappointed, and said that she should have done better in French, and so on. My response was, 'I don't really care how you did in French. I think you're fantastic. In fact, I wouldn't really care if your whole report was bad, I love you because I love you.' Later that evening, as I thought about our conversation, I sensed God saying to me, 'This is how I feel about you.'

The love of God for each one of us is far greater than the love of human parents for their children. I often feel that I could do better, that I am not good at one thing or another, and that I fail again and again. Yet God accepts us and loves us simply because he loves us. We know this because the Spirit of God witnesses to us – both objectively through an ongoing change in our character and in our relationships, and subjectively through a deep inner conviction that we are children of God.

In these ways (the word of God, the work of Jesus and the witness of the Spirit), those who believe in Jesus can be sure that they are children of God and that they have eternal life.

It is not arrogant to be sure that we have eternal life. It is based on what God has promised, on what Jesus died to achieve, and on the work of the Holy Spirit in our lives. It is one of the privileges of being a child of God that we can be absolutely confident about our relationship with our Father, that we can know his forgiveness and be sure that we are Christians and that we have eternal life.

If you are unsure about whether you have ever really believed in Jesus, here is a prayer that you can pray as a way of starting the Christian life and receiving all the benefits which Christ died to make possible.

> Heavenly Father, I am sorry for the things I have done wrong in my life. [Take a few moments to ask his forgiveness for anything particular that is on your conscience.] Please forgive me. I now turn from everything that I know is wrong.

> Thank you that you sent your Son, Jesus, to die on the cross for me so that I could be forgiven and set free. From now on I will follow and obey him as my Lord.

> Thank you that you now offer me this gift of forgiveness and your Spirit. I now receive that gift.

> Please come into my life by your Holy Spirit to be with me for ever. Through Jesus Christ, our Lord. Amen.

Endnotes

1. Lesslie Newbigin, *Foolishness to the Greeks* (SPCK, 1986), p.127.
2. C. S. Lewis, *The Last Battle* (HarperCollins, 2008 reprint), p.222.

Alpha

Alpha is a practical introduction to the Christian faith, initiated by HTB in London and now being run by thousands of churches, of many denominations, throughout the world. If you are interested in finding out more about the Christian faith and would like details of your nearest Alpha, please visit our website:

alpha.org

or contact:
The Alpha Office,
HTB Brompton Road,
London,
SW7 1JA

Tel: 0845 644 7544

Alpha titles available

Why Jesus?   A booklet – given to all participants at the start of Alpha. 'The clearest, best illustrated and most challenging short presentation of Jesus that I know.' – Michael Green

Why Christmas?   The Christmas version of *Why Jesus?*

Questions of Life   Alpha in book form. In fifteen compelling chapters Nicky Gumbel points the way to an authentic Christianity which is exciting and relevant to today's world.

Searching Issues   The seven issues most often raised by participants on Alpha, including, suffering, other religions, science and Christianity, and the Trinity.

A Life Worth Living   What happens after Alpha? Based on the book of Philippians, this is an invaluable next step for those who have just completed Alpha, and for anyone eager to put their faith on a firm biblical footing.

The Jesus Lifestyle   Studies in the Sermon on the Mount showing how Jesus' teaching flies in the face of a modern lifestyle and presents us with a radical alternative.

30 Days   Nicky Gumbel selects thirty passages from the Old and New Testament which can be read over thirty days. It is designed for those on Alpha and others who are interested in beginning to explore the Bible.

All titles are by Nicky Gumbel,
who is vicar of Holy Trinity Brompton

About the Author

Nicky Gumbel is the pioneer of Alpha. He read law at Cambridge and theology at Oxford, practised as a barrister and is now vicar of HTB in London. He is the author of many bestselling books about the Christian faith, including *Questions of Life*, *The Jesus Lifestyle*, *Why Jesus?*, *A Life Worth Living*, *Searching Issues* and *30 Days*.